TURNING POINTS IN U.S. HISTORY

LOUISIANA PURCHASE

by Christopher Forest

pogo

Ideas for Parents and Teachers

Pogo Books let children practice reading informational text while introducing them to nonfiction features such as headings, labels, sidebars, maps, and diagrams, as well as a table of contents, glossary, and index.

Carefully leveled text with a strong photo match offers early fluent readers the support they need to succeed.

Before Reading

- "Walk" through the book and point out the various nonfiction features. Ask the student what purpose each feature serves.
- Look at the glossary together. Read and discuss the words.

Read the Book

- Have the child read the book independently.
- Invite him or her to list questions that arise from reading.

After Reading

- Discuss the child's questions. Talk about how he or she might find answers to those questions.
- Prompt the child to think more. Ask: What did you know about the Louisiana Purchase before reading this book? What more would you like to learn?

Pogo Books are published by Jump!
5357 Penn Avenue South
Minneapolis, MN 55419
www.jumplibrary.com

Library of Congress Cataloging-in-Publication Data

Names: Forest, Christopher, author.
Title: Louisiana Purchase / by Christopher Forest.
Description: Minneapolis, MN: Pogo Books; [2021]
Series: Turning points in U.S. history
Includes index.
Audience: Ages 7-10 | Audience: Grades 2-3
Identifiers: LCCN 2019046347 (print)
LCCN 2019046348 (ebook)
ISBN 9781645274346 (hardcover)
ISBN 9781645274353 (paperback)
ISBN 9781645274360 (ebook)
Subjects: LCSH: Louisiana Purchase—Juvenile literature.
United States—Territorial expansion—History—19th century—Juvenile literature.
Classification: LCC E333 .F67 2021 (print)
LCC E333 (ebook)
DDC 973.4/6—dc23
LC record available at https://lccn.loc.gov/2019046347
LC ebook record available at https://lccn.loc.gov/2019046348

Editor: Jenna Gleisner
Designer: Jenna Casura

Photo Credits: Bettmann/Getty, cover; GraphicaArtis/Getty, 1; agefotostock/Alamy, 3; Everett Historical/Shutterstock, 4, 8, 14-15, 18-19; PRISMA ARCHIVO/Alamy, 5; Pictorial Press Ltd/Alamy, 6-7; Ed Vebell/Getty, 9; Pictures Now/Alamy, 10-11; AMERICAN PHILOSOPHICAL SOCIETY/Science Source, 12-13; Everett Collection/Age Fotostock, 14; ClassicStock/Alamy, 16; Kean Collection/Getty, 17; iStock, 20-21; North Wind Picture Archives/Alamy, 23.

Printed in the United States of America at Corporate Graphics in North Mankato, Minnesota.

TABLE OF CONTENTS

CHAPTER 1
The Country Grows.......4

CHAPTER 2
Exploring the Land.......8

CHAPTER 3
What a Deal!.......16

QUICK FACTS & TOOLS
Timeline.......22
Glossary.......23
Index.......24
To Learn More.......24

CHAPTER 1

THE COUNTRY GROWS

November 15, 1805, was an important day. Why? **Explorers** Meriwether Lewis and William Clark arrived at the Pacific Ocean. They had been traveling for about 550 days.

Meriwether Lewis

They started in St. Louis, Missouri. Why did they go? The United States had bought the Louisiana **Territory**. They were sent to explore this new land.

Thomas Jefferson was president in 1803. He bought the territory from France. Why? He wanted to control the **port** city of New Orleans. He also wanted to find a **Northwest Passage** to the Pacific Ocean.

The country's **population** was growing, too. Jefferson felt the country needed more space. It would help make the country strong. This idea became known as **Manifest Destiny**.

TAKE A LOOK!

The Louisiana Territory began at the Mississippi River. It went west to the Rocky Mountains. Take a look!

CHAPTER 2

EXPLORING THE LAND

Jefferson hired Lewis to explore and map the land. Lewis hired his friend Clark to help.

The men formed a team of around 45 explorers. They were called the **Corps** of Discovery. They left St. Louis on May 14, 1804.

They met with around 50 Native American tribes. These tribes lived in the territory. They had lived there for centuries. Some helped the corps. They gave them food or horses. One was Sacagawea. She helped guide the men.

Sacagawea

and Clark Codices.
C.– Clark.
Journal
Clark Codices.
A.– Clark.
Journal
May 13, 1804 – Aug. 14, 1804.
(complete.)
Clark's No. 1
Biddle's No 1
Coues' A.
pages 184
Folios 92
Codex Aa
American Philosophical Society,
(FOUNDED 1743,)
104 SOUTH FIFTH STREET,
PHILADELPHIA.

Lewis and Clark traveled nearly 8,000 miles (12,875 kilometers)! They mapped the land. They **identified** 178 plants and 122 animals. They wrote about them in journals. They drew pictures, too.

WHAT DO YOU THINK?

Lewis and Clark saw many animals they'd never seen before. These included bison and rattlesnakes. They saw prairie dogs and grizzly bears, too! What would it be like to see an unfamiliar animal?

Lewis and Clark reached the Pacific coast. Then they turned around. They returned to St. Louis. They got there on September 23, 1806. They had not found a Northwest Passage. But they had learned a lot about the territory. They had made many maps.

map created by Lewis and Clark

CHAPTER 3

WHAT A DEAL!

The Louisiana Territory cost 15 million dollars. That would be about 305 million dollars today. It was a good deal! The United States now owned the Mississippi River. People traveled along it. They **traded** goods as they went.

The country also gained the city of New Orleans. It was at the mouth of the Mississippi River. Other countries traded goods here.

Thousands of people moved to the Louisiana Territory in the 1800s. Many started farms on the **Great Plains**.

DID YOU KNOW?

The Louisiana Purchase wasn't good for everyone. No one asked Native Americans about it. When Americans moved west, they took land from them.

The Louisiana Purchase changed the United States forever. The country doubled in size. It shaped the country into what it is today.

WHAT DO YOU THINK?

Where do you live? Is it part of what was the Louisiana Territory? How would the country be different if the United States hadn't purchased the land? How would your life be different?

QUICK FACTS & TOOLS

TIMELINE

1803
The United States takes control of the Louisiana Territory in December.

1804
Jefferson sends Lewis and Clark to explore the Louisiana Territory in May.

1805
Lewis and Clark reach the Pacific coast in November.

1806
Lewis and Clark return from their voyage after two years, four months, and 10 days. They share their findings.

1812
Louisiana becomes the 18th state. It is the first state in the Louisiana Territory.

1840
Nearly 7 million Americans live west of the Appalachian Mountains, many in the Louisiana Territory.

GLOSSARY

corps: A group of people.

explorers: People who travel and look around in order to discover things.

Great Plains: A large, flat area of the central United States and western Canada that is covered in grasslands.

identified: Established the identity of.

Manifest Destiny: The belief that the United States had to grow west.

Northwest Passage: An all-water route across North America.

population: The total number of people who live in a place.

port: A harbor where ships can load and unload goods.

territory: A large region of land.

traded: Gave something in exchange for another.

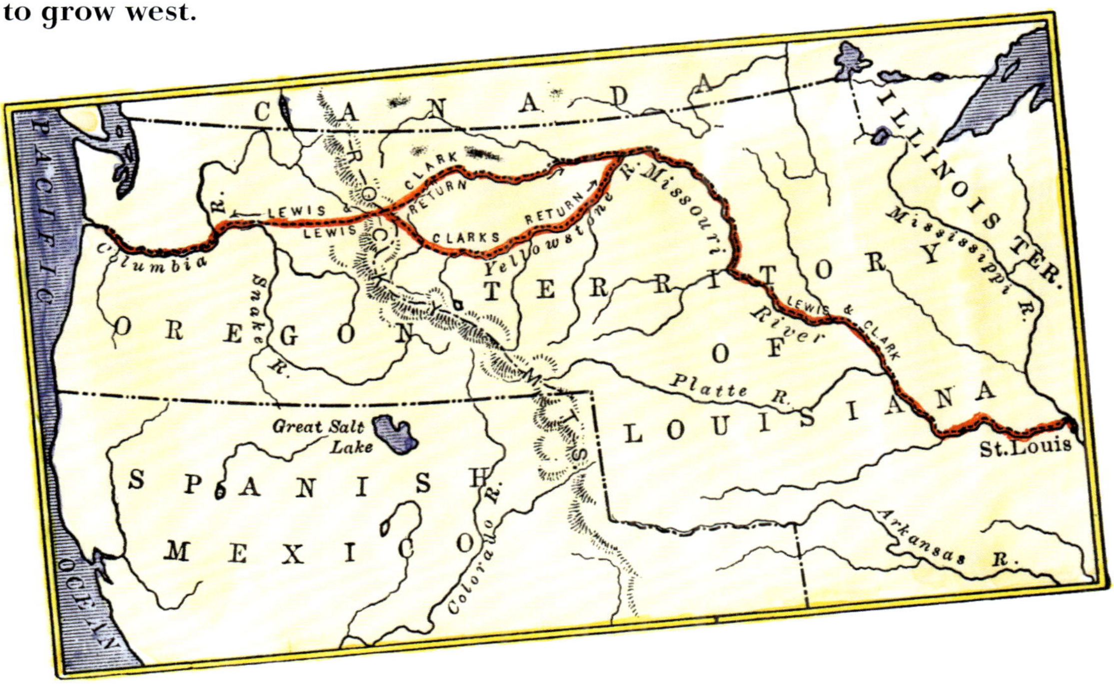

INDEX

animals 13
Clark, William 4, 8, 13, 14
Corps of Discovery 9
farms 18
France 6
Great Plains 18
Jefferson, Thomas 6, 8
journals 13
Lewis, Meriwether 4, 8, 13, 14
Louisiana Purchase 18, 21
Louisiana Territory 5, 6, 7, 10, 14, 16, 18, 21
Manifest Destiny 6
map 8, 13, 14
Mississippi River 7, 16, 17
Native American tribes 10, 18
New Orleans 6, 7, 17
Northwest Passage 6, 14
Pacific Ocean 4, 6, 7
plants 13
population 6
Rocky Mountains 7
Sacagawea 10
St. Louis, Missouri 5, 9, 14
traded 16, 17

TO LEARN MORE

Finding more information is as easy as 1, 2, 3.

1. Go to www.factsurfer.com
2. Enter "LouisianaPurchase" into the search box.
3. Choose your book to see a list of websites.

FACT SURFER